HOW TO MAKE HOLIDAY

POP-UPS

By Joan Irvine
Illustrated by Linda Hendry

Morrow Junior Books
New York

Text copyright © 1996 by Joan Irvine
Illustrations copyright © 1996 by Linda Hendry

First published in Canada in 1995 by Kids Can Press, 29 Birch Avenue,
Toronto, Canada M4V 1E2.

Printed in the United States of America.

1 2 3 4 5 6 7 8 9 10

Library of Congress Cataloging-in-Publication Data
Irvine, Joan.
How to make holiday pop-ups/by Joan Irvine;
illustrated by Linda Hendry.
p. cm.
Summary: Provides instructions for making pop-ups for special events,
particularly holidays that kids are involved in celebrating and for which
they exchange cards.
ISBN 0-688-13608-7 (trade)—ISBN 0-688-13609-5 (library)
1. Paper work—Juvenile literature.   2. Paper toy making—Juvenile
literature.   3. Holiday decorations—Juvenile literature.   [1. Paper work.
2. Handicraft.   3. Paper toy making.   4. Toy making.   5. Holiday
decorations.]   I. Hendry, Linda, ill.   II. Title.   TT870.I79 1996
745.594'1—dc20   95-35174   CIP AC

Contents

As always, I dedicate this book to my family,
especially my mother, Dr. Norma Hopkinson,
who has always shown so much love and
enthusiasm for me and my work over the years.

Acknowledgments

I would like to thank the many people who were so generous with their time and information. Some of the people and organizations that were very helpful include: Dr. Mohammad Ashraf, Director of the Islamic Society of North America; Don Baldwin, Royal Canadian Legion; the Buddhist Association of Canada; Rabbi Burnstein; Bhaktimarga Swami of the Hare Krishna Temple; the Canadian Macedonian Place; Nasser Danesh, Department of Middle East and Islamic Studies, University of Toronto; Rabbi Dratch, Shaarei Shomayim Congregation; Kamal Gillani of the Iranian Community Association of Ontario; the Hindu Temple Society of Canada; Grant Ikuta of the Toronto Buddhist Church; Islamic Books; the Japanese Information Centre of the Consulate General of Japan; Father John K. S. Koulouras of the All Saints Greek Orthodox Church and Cultural Centre; Lenore Keeshig-Tobias, Ojibwe author; Steven Ma, Executive Director of the Chinese Information and Community Services; the Mexican Consulate; the Ontario Black History Society; Brit Regan of the Bahá'í National Centre; Nachhattar Singh, priest at Shromani Sikh Sangat; Jagan Nath Sharma, Hindu minister; Dr. Ron Sunter, Historical Department, University of Guelph; and Shirley Uldall, Centre for South Asian Studies, University of Toronto. Other individuals who helped immensely include: Ariel Barkley, Sarita and Subash Chaddah, Maria Gavaris, Freida Gilson, Bill Hawkes, John Hoita, Mary Hopkinson, Gerry Parkhill, Kris Sharma, Ruth Tupper, and Sikander and Dolores Umar.

Finally, I would like to thank my husband, Steve, and my children, Seth and Elly, for their patience and understanding during busy times; my editor, Liz MacLeod, for her warmth, hard work and good humor; my illustrator, Linda Hendry, for her wonderful illustrations; my designer, Karen Powers, for fitting everything in so beautifully; and my publishers, Valerie Hussey and Ricky Englander, for their support in this project.

Introduction

Since writing *How to Make Pop-ups* and *How to Make Super Pop-ups*, I've had a lot of fun teaching people to make pop-ups. One thing I've noticed is kids especially like to make pop-up cards to celebrate special events. If you've ever wanted to make a special holiday card to send to a friend or relative, then this is the book for you.

There are far too many wonderful holidays from around the world to fit in just one book. I decided to look for the holidays kids are really involved in celebrating and ones for which people exchange cards. I felt like a detective tracking down the many different special days. I talked to experts from many different cultures and I learned so much researching this book — it has been my most challenging project ever and one of my most rewarding.

During my research, I was fascinated by the similarities between different cultures. For instance, people throughout the world believe fire and light are very important for celebrations. Something else all cultures share is a desire for love, friendship and peace. I hope as you read about holidays around the world and make pop-up cards to celebrate them you'll also learn to understand and care about people around the world.

I've included as many holidays as I can in this book and I've given ideas at the end of each chapter on how you can change cards to make others for more holidays. I hope every holiday that's important to you is in this book. However, if you can't find your favorite holiday, then adapt a card to make your own special one. Have fun making pop-up cards for holidays from around the world!

Materials

To make your holiday pop-up cards, you will need the following materials.

Paper   For pop-ups that will last, use heavy paper such as construction paper or light bristol board. Lighter weight paper can be used for pop-ups that don't get much wear and tear. The instructions will tell you when to use bristol board or cardboard.

Scissors   A sharp pair of scissors with pointed ends are good for cutting paper. Remember to use all cutting equipment with care.

Cutting blade   A utility knife or any other kind of craft knife is useful for making a cut in the middle of a page. Ask an adult to help when you need to use a cutting blade.

Ruler   Use a ruler for measurements given in the instructions. A metal ruler will help you make crisp folds and guide your cutting blade.

Glue   With light paper, use a glue stick. With heavy paper, you can use white glue. Always apply glue sparingly and keep glue away from all moving parts of your pop-up. When you glue two pieces of paper together, a thin line of glue on each side is usually enough.

Pencils, markers, crayons, colored pencils, paints Use an erasable pencil for marking measurements and for designing your drawings. Then go over your pencil drawings with color.

String, rubber bands, fabrics, buttons, ribbons, gift wrap, feathers, pictures from magazines These materials and others can be glued to your pop-ups as decorations.

Symbols and Definitions

The following symbols and definitions will be useful to you when you use this book.

Tab A small paper insert that can be glued or pulled

Sliding strip A small piece of paper that helps an object to move

Mountain fold
An upward fold, shaped like a mountain

Valley fold
A downward fold, shaped like a valley

Accordion fold
An up-down-up fold or a down-up-down fold, shaped like a fan

Fold line — — — — — — — —

Cut line —————————————

Draw

Color

Glue

Measure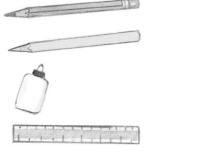

Tips for Folding and Scoring

- To make a straight fold on heavy paper, score the paper first. Scoring means making a crease on your paper along the line to be folded. Lay a metal ruler near the line to be folded. Then carefully run the blunt end of a pair of scissors or a ballpoint pen without ink along the fold line. Some people score their paper by running a fingernail along the fold line. When you fold your paper, remember to press firmly.

Tips for Cutting

- You will need a sharp pair of scissors for most activities in this book. If you are making a cut in the middle of a page, use a pair of pointed scissors to puncture one of the corners of the cut line before cutting.

- A cutting blade, such as a utility knife, works best to make a cut in the middle of a page. Be careful when using a cutting blade. Adult supervision is recommended.

- When you use a cutting blade, use a metal ruler to help you guide the knife in a straight line. Always put a board or a thick piece of cardboard under your work, so you don't damage your work space.

Tips for Measuring

- All measurements are given in both metric and British imperial systems. When you follow the instructions for making the pop-ups, start with one system and stay with it for the whole activity. Measurements differ slightly from system to system.

Part One

Celebrate friendship and love

Friendship and love are important to everybody, no matter what culture. One of the best ways to make someone feel special is to send a card you made yourself. With the ideas here you can make a one-of-a-kind valentine or give your parents an original card on Mother's or Father's Day. You'll also find out how to celebrate the Bahá'í holiday Ayyám-i-Há, discover what a *martinki* is and learn how to make a *rakhi* bracelet for a Hindu holiday.

There are many other holidays related to friendship and love. You could send your grandparents a pop-up card on Grandparents' Day, the first Sunday after Labor Day. Tibetan Buddhists observe December 25 as Children's Day and the United Nations celebrates Universal Children's Day on the first Monday in October. You could use the ideas in this chapter to make cards for any of these — why not make some with a friend?

Celebrate Valentine's Day

February 14

On Valentine's Day, people give each other cards, flowers, candies and other gifts. This holiday is often called St. Valentine's Day and honors two men, both named Valentine, who lived in Rome over 1700 years ago. Traditional symbols for Valentine's Day are hearts, cupids, flowers and kisses.

1 Take two pieces of paper, each 21.5 cm x 28 cm (8½ in. x 11 in.). Fold each paper in half. Put one paper aside.

2 On the folded edge of the other paper, mark a dot 3 cm (1⅛ in.) from the top edge of the paper. Starting from this dot, draw nine more dots that are 1.6 cm (⅝ in.) apart on the folded edge.

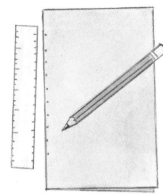

3 Using a ruler, draw a straight line 5 cm (2 in.) long, starting from the first dot and moving away from the fold. Draw lines 5 cm (2 in.) long from all the other dots. Keep them as parallel to each other as possible.

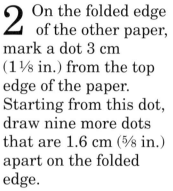

4 Shade in the space between every second pair of lines as shown.

5 Draw dotted lines between the lines as shown. The dotted lines that are not at the ends of the solid lines are 3 cm (1⅛ in.) from the folded edge. Do not draw dotted lines on the shaded areas.

6 Cut the solid lines as far as the dotted lines. Fold the cut strips forward and then fold them back again.

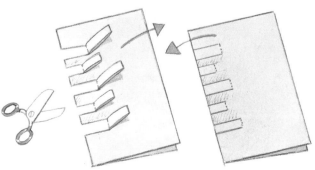

7 Open your card and hold it like a tent. Push the strips through to the other side of your paper. Close your paper and press firmly. Open to see the pop-up strips.

8 Take a pink strip of paper, 15 cm x 6 cm (6 in. x 2¼ in.). Fold the strip into thirds so each section is 5 cm (2 in.) long. Then fold the strip in half again. Draw half a heart along the folded edge as shown and cut it out. You now have three pink hearts.

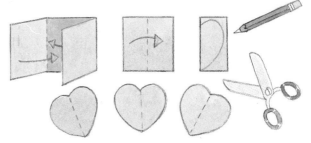

9 Cut a strip of red paper, 7.5 cm x 4 cm (3 in. x 1½ in.). Fold the strip in half end to end. Then fold the strip in half again. Draw half a heart along the folded edge and cut it out. You now have two red hearts.

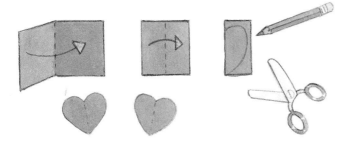

10 Apply a small amount of glue to the fold on the top strip of your paper. Place a pink heart on the fold, matching the fold lines of the heart with the fold lines of the strip. Attach pink hearts to the middle strip and the bottom strip in the same way.

11 Attach the red hearts to the remaining strips in the same way.

12 Apply glue to the back of your paper but not in the area of the pop-up strips. Place the glued paper on the paper you put aside, which now becomes the outside of your card. Write a message to your valentine inside the card, then decorate the inside and outside.

Celebrate Mother's Day

Second Sunday in May

Mother's Day is a day to honor mothers. Celebrating Mom with a special day began in 1907 in the United States and soon the custom spread.

---

1 Take two different colored pieces of paper, each 21.5 cm x 28 cm (8 ½ in. x 11 in.). Fold each paper in half. Put one aside.

2 Place the other paper so the folded edge is on your left. Mark a dot 9 cm (3 ½ in.) from the bottom of the paper. Mark another dot 14 cm (5 ½ in.) from the bottom of the paper. Mark a third dot 19 cm (7 ½ in.) from the bottom of the paper.

3 From each dot draw a diagonal line 2.5 cm (1 in.). The lines should be parallel to each other. Cut the three lines, starting from the folded edge.

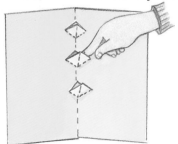

4 Fold the cut strips forward and then fold them back again.

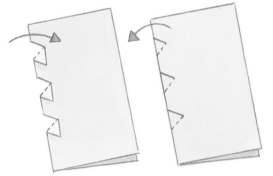

5 Open your paper. To make the cut sections pop out, pull the shapes toward you and press along the fold lines. The cut sections will stand out toward you.

6 Cut three green strips of paper, each 7.5 cm x 1.2 cm (3 in. x ½ in.). These will be the stems. Apply glue to the bottom of each strip. Place the strips on the pop-up sections as shown and press firmly.

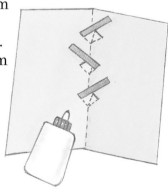

7 To make flowers, take three colored squares of paper, each 6 cm x 6 cm (2 ¼ in. x 2 ¼ in.). Draw and cut out a flower from each one. Glue a flower to the end of each stem. Close your paper. If any part of the flower sticks out from your paper, cut it smaller or change its position on its stem.

8 Apply glue to the back of your paper but not in the area of the pop-up strips. Place the glued paper on the paper you put aside, which now becomes the outside of your card. Write a message inside the card, then decorate the inside and outside.

Celebrate Father's Day

Third Sunday in June

The origins of Father's Day aren't known for certain but most people agree that it was probably started over 80 years ago in Spokane, Washington, by Mrs. Bruce Dodd.

1 Follow steps 1 to 6 of the Mother's Day card. You can make the strips of paper in step 6 any color you like.

2 Take three squares of white paper. On each one, draw a member of your family or anything you think your dad will like. Color and cut out your pictures and attach them to the paper strips as in step 7, then follow step 8 and decorate your card.

Celebrate Ayyám-i-Há

Begins after sunset on February 26 and continues until sunset on March 1

Ayyám-i-Há means "days of generosity" and is a Bahá'í holiday. It is a time for kindness and the giving of small gifts as well as a time to prepare for the Nineteen Day Fast, which begins March 2. People of the Bahá'í faith follow the teachings of the prophet Bahá'u'lláh. The idea of unity is very important to the five million Bahá'ís around the world.

1 Fold in half a piece of paper, 21.5 cm x 28 cm (8 ½ in. x 11 in.). Open it again and put it aside.

2 Take a piece of white paper, 28 cm x 11 cm (11 in. x 4 ¼ in.). Fold it in half crosswise. Then fold it in half crosswise again.

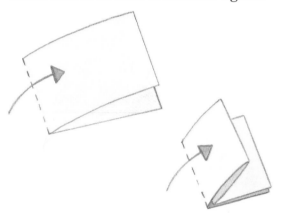

3 Draw a child on the top section of the folded strip as shown. Make sure the hands and feet of your figure run off both sides, so your figures in each section will be connected.

4 Cut out the figure and open the strip. Draw and color the children. Bend the fold lines so the middle folds are mountain folds. Bend the other folds so they are valley folds (see page 6).

12

5 Fold the figures together again. Apply glue on the back of the far left child and place it as shown on the left side of the paper from step 1.

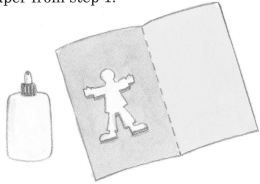

6 Apply glue on the back of the far right figure. Close your card and press firmly. The far right figure will now be glued to the right side of your card. Allow the glue to dry.

7 Take a colored piece of paper, 12.5 cm x 28 cm (5 in. x 11 in.). Fold it in half as shown. Then fold it in half again. Draw the following pattern on the paper. Cut it out.

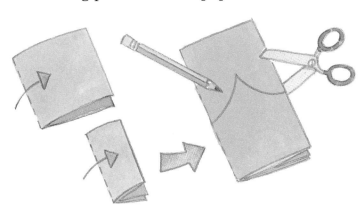

8 Decorate each piece with markers. You can also add glitter and sequins. Fold the strips so the middle fold is a mountain fold. Fold the side folds into valley folds.

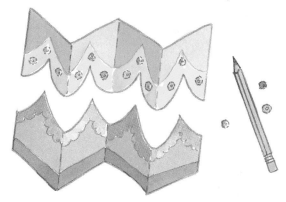

9 Take one of the strips and apply glue on the back at the ends. Carefully place the glued areas on each side of the card as shown. The middle section should stand out. Repeat the same steps with the other strip of paper.

10 Take a small piece of paper and write "Happy Ayyám-i-Há!" on it. Fold it in half and glue it onto the top strip of paper. Make sure you match the folds. Decorate the inside and outside of your card.

More holidays

Prvi Mart is celebrated by Macedonians on March 1. They give gifts called *martinki*, which are tiny red and white doll pins, tassels or bracelets. Some people also throw threads to swallows building nests.

1 Turn to the Halloween card on page 56 and follow steps 1 to 5, using any color of paper you like. Make a bird's head around the pop-up shape. Follow step 9, but write "Vesel Prvi Mart" inside.

2 To make a bracelet, twist together a white piece of wool and red piece of wool, each 30 cm (12 in.) long. Tie a knot at each end. Tape the bracelet to the inside of the bird's beak.

Raksha Bandhan is a Hindu holiday in August celebrated by brothers and sisters. Hindu girls and women tie bracelets called *rakhi* on their brothers' arms, and their brothers promise to help and protect them.

1 Turn to the Earth Day card on page 60 and follow steps 1 to 7.

2 To make the bracelet, braid skeins of red, yellow and gold (or green) embroidery thread. Tie the ends together. Make a flower out of gold and red paper and glue it to the middle of the bracelet.

3 Tape the bracelet to the card. Follow step 10, but write "Many Happy Returns on Raksha Bandhan" inside.

Part Two

Celebrate your heritage

It's fun to talk to your parents and grandparents and find out about your family's past. Together you can look at old photos, try out recipes that have been handed down from generation to generation and even learn about your ancestors' lives in other countries. In this chapter you'll discover harvest holidays, celebrate the country you live in, read about a holiday just for girls and more.

There are lots of heritage holidays. You can celebrate Black History Month in February, the Scandinavian holiday of St. Lucia Day on December 13 and the Welsh St. David's Day on March 1. Those are just a few — you may discover many more as you find out about your own heritage.

Celebrate Independence Day

July 4

On Independence Day, people in the United States celebrate with fireworks, parades, cookouts, sports and citizenship ceremonies. The first celebration of this day was on July 4, 1776, when the American colonies declared independence from Great Britain.

1 Fold in half a piece of paper, 21.5 cm x 28 cm (8 ½ in. x 11 in.). Place your paper so the fold line is on the left. On the fold line, mark a dot 5 cm (2 in.) from the top of the paper. Mark a second dot at the top of the paper 8 cm (3 ⅛ in.) to the right of the fold. Draw a line between the dots. Fold the top left corner forward along the line. Open your paper and put it aside.

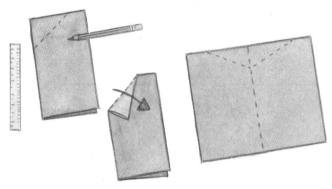

2 To make the fireworks, take another piece of paper, 18 cm x 18 cm (7 ¼ in. x 7 ¼ in.). Fold it in half and place it so the folded edge is on your left.

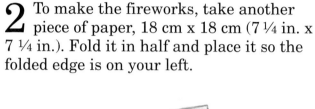

3 Mark a dot on the folded edge, 14 cm (5 ½ in.) up from the bottom of the paper. Mark a second dot on the bottom of the paper, 4 cm (1 ½ in.) from the fold.

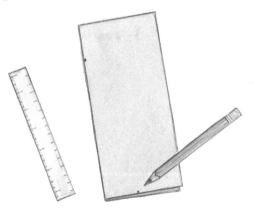

4 Between these two dots, draw the following shape. Cut out the shape.

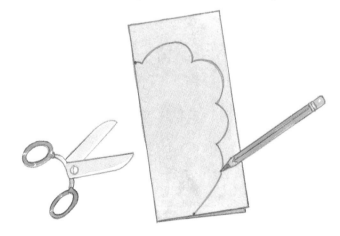

5 Fold the bottom edge up 1.2 cm (½ in.). Fold it back to its original position.

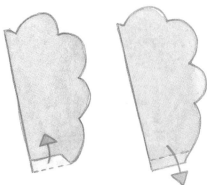

6 Open the fireworks shape. Mark a dot where the fold lines meet. Draw a little triangle with the dot at its top and cut it out. You now have two tabs on the shape.

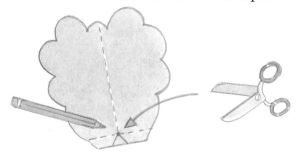

7 Take small squares of foil or paper. Draw and cut out stars. Glue them onto the fireworks shape. You can glue stars to the edge of the shape, but don't glue them on the fold lines.

8 Fold back the tabs on the fireworks shape. Apply glue on the bottom of each tab.

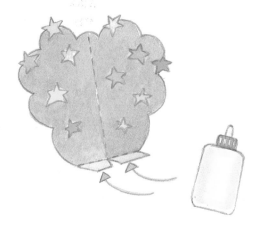

9 Fit the fireworks shape around the triangle on your base paper. Glue the tabs of your fireworks shape along the triangle lines of your card base. Make sure the fold lines of your fireworks line up with the fold lines of the card.

10 Write "Happy Independence Day" inside your card, then decorate the inside and the outside.

Celebrate Thanksgiving

Usually the fourth Thursday in November

Thanksgiving is a time of feasting and giving thanks for the harvest. The first Thanksgiving was celebrated by Native Americans and Pilgrims in 1621. Most foods eaten at Thanksgiving were originally grown only in North America. Native Americans introduced the Pilgrims to cranberries, corn, pumpkins, beans and many other foods.

1 Take two pieces of paper, each 21.5 cm x 28 cm (8 ½ in. x 11 in.). Fold each paper in half. Put one aside.

2 Place the other paper so the folded edge is on your left. Mark a dot on the folded edge, 7 cm (2 ¾ in.) from the bottom of the paper. Mark a dot on the top edge, 7 cm (2 ¾ in.) from the top right corner. Draw a dotted line between the two dots.

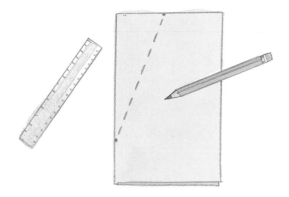

3 Take the top left corner and fold it down along the dotted line.

4 Mark a dot on the folded edge of the triangle fold, 10 cm (4 in.) up from the tip of the triangle fold. Draw a curved line from the dot to the folded edge as shown.

5 Cut the line, cutting through all layers of paper.

6 Unfold the cut section so it is back in its original position. Now draw a line that joins the bottom of the fold line with the bottom of the cut line. Fold the cut section forward along this line. Unfold the section and open the card. This shape will be your turkey feathers — draw and color feathers on it.

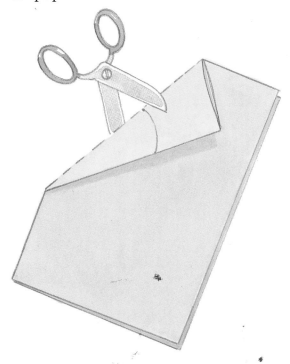

7 To make the turkey's head and body, fold in half a piece of paper, 16 cm x 16 cm (6 ¼ in. x 6 ¼ in.). Draw or trace the shape at the bottom of the page along the folded edge. Draw the short dotted line where shown. Cut out the shape.

8 Open the shape and bend the head of the turkey forward along the dotted line. Draw on details such as eyes and a beak. Cut a wattle out of red paper, fold it in half, then open it and glue it under the turkey's beak.

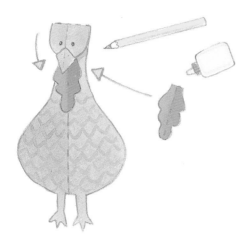

9 Apply glue to the back of the turkey. Match the folds of the turkey to the folds of the feathers and press firmly. Glue the head to the neck to hold it in place.

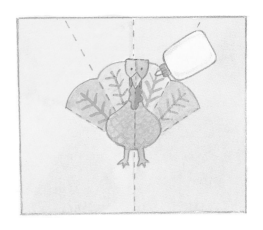

10 Open your paper and hold it like a tent. Push the cut piece down in the opposite direction of the fold, so it is pushed through to the other side of the paper. Close the paper and press firmly. When you open your paper, the turkey will pop up.

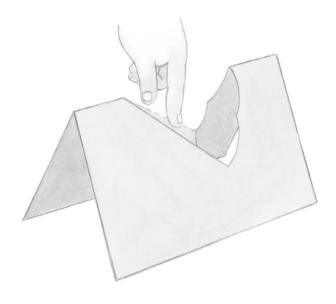

11 Apply glue to the back of your paper but not in the area of the pop-up. Place the glued paper on the paper you put aside, which now becomes the outside of your card. Write "Happy Thanksgiving" inside your card, then decorate the inside and outside.

Celebrate Kwanzaa

From December 26 to January 1

Kwanzaa is a family event that lasts for seven days and is celebrated by more than five million people of African descent. It is based on traditional African values and harvest festivals and was created in the United States in 1966 by Dr. Maulana Karenga. Kwanzaa means "first fruits" in the East African language of Swahili.

1 Take two pieces of paper, each 21.5 cm x 28 cm (8 ½ in. x 11 in.). Fold each paper in half. Put one paper aside.

2 Place the other paper so the folded edge is at the top. On the fold, mark two dots, each one 5 cm (2 in.) from the ends.

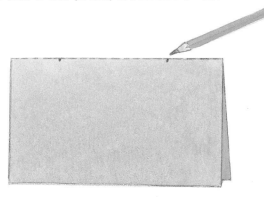

3 Draw two parallel lines down from the dots. Each line should be 4 cm (1 ½ in.) long. Cut the lines, starting from the folded edge.

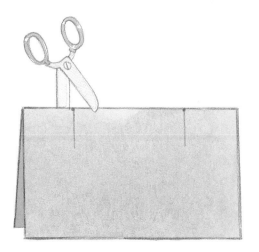

4 Fold the cut strip forward and then fold it back to its original position.

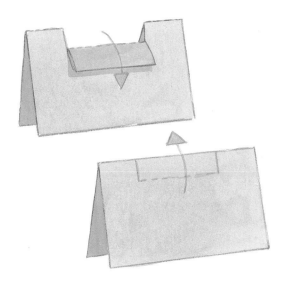

21

5 Open your paper and hold it like a tent. Push the strip down in the opposite direction of the fold, so it is pushed through to the other side of your paper. Close the paper and press firmly. Open to see the pop-up strip.

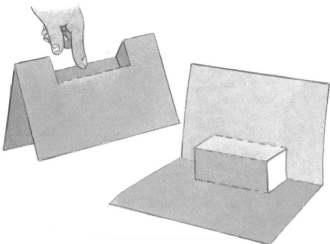

6 Close your paper. On the folded edge of the pop-up strip, mark two dots, each one 4.5 cm (1 ¾ in.) from the ends.

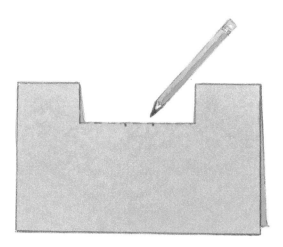

7 Draw two parallel lines down from the dots. Each line should be 2 cm (¾ in.) long. Starting from the folded edge, cut the lines, being careful to cut through only the top fold of your paper. Do not cut through both folded edges of the pop-up strip.

8 Fold the cut strip forward and then fold it back to its original position. Open your paper and push the strip down and through to the other side of your paper. Close the paper and press firmly. Open to see the second pop-up strip. The two pop-up strips are your Kwanzaa table.

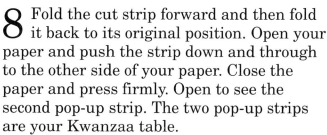

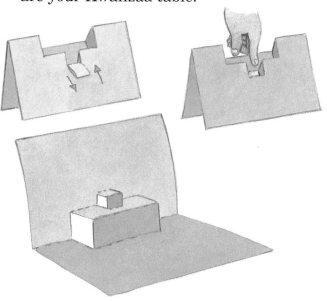

9 Now make the symbols of Kwanzaa. To make the candleholder *(kinara)*, take a piece of heavy paper, 10 cm x 5 cm (4 in. x 2 in.), and fold it in half. Place it so the folded edge is on your left. Draw or trace the following pattern on the paper, starting at the folded edge. Cut it out. Then make seven candles *(mishumaa saba)*, each 2 cm (¾ in.) long. There should be one black, three green and three red candles. Cut seven small yellow candle flames and glue them to the top of the candles. Apply glue to the bottom of the candles and glue them to the candleholder as shown.

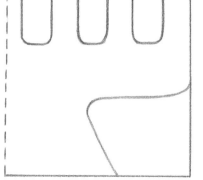

10 Draw, color and cut out these other Kwanzaa symbols.

Straw mat *(mkeka)* — represents tradition
Ears of corn *(muhindi)* — as many ears as there are children in the family
Unity Cup *(kikombe cha umoja)* — one large cup that everyone drinks from
Crops *(mazeo)* — fruit and vegetables
Gifts *(zawad)* (optional) — a drum or a book

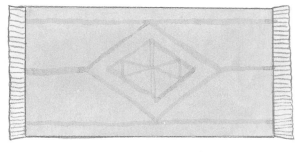

11 Glue the candleholder with candles to the middle pop-up strip. Then glue the straw mat onto the middle of the table. Glue the other objects as shown.

12 Apply glue to the back of your paper but not in the area of the pop-up table. Place the glued paper on the paper you put aside, which now becomes the outside of your card. Write "Happy Kwanzaa" inside the card, then decorate the inside and outside.

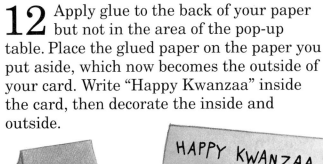

Celebrate Diwali

October or November

Diwali is a Hindu festival of lights. It marks the beginning of winter and the end of the harvest season in India. During Diwali the Hindu goddess of wealth, Lakshmi, is welcomed to homes by *dipa,* which means "light." The light comes from an oil-filled saucer with a cotton wick. Diwali is celebrated in many countries by Hindus, Jains and Sikhs.

1 Take two pieces of paper, each 21.5 cm x 28 cm (8 ½ in. x 11 in.). Fold each paper in half. Put one aside.

2 Place the other paper so the folded edge is on your left. From the folded edge, draw two lines as shown. The top line should be 5 cm (2 in.) long and the bottom line should be 1.2 cm (½ in.) long. The lines should be 3 cm (1⅛ in.) apart.

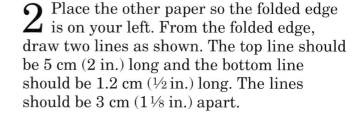

3 Cut the two lines, starting from the folded edge. Fold the cut section forward and then fold it back to its original position.

4 Open your paper and hold it like a tent. Push the strip through to the other side of your paper. Close the paper and press firmly, then open it to see the pop-up shape.

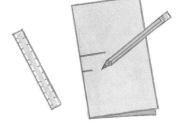

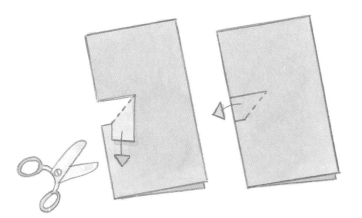

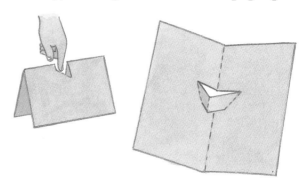

5 Draw the following lines around the pop-up to create a dipa and then color it. To make coloring it easier, slide a piece of paper through the cut section of the dipa.

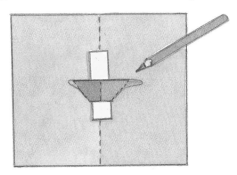

6 Apply glue to the back of your paper. Do not apply glue in the area of the pop-up dipa. Place the glued paper on the paper you put aside, which now becomes the outside of your card.

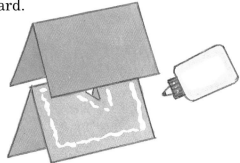

7 Color the inside of the dipa. You can draw and color a small pool of oil inside the bottom area of the dipa.

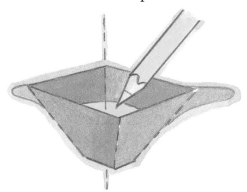

8 To make the flame of the dipa, take a yellow piece of paper, 4 cm x 4 cm (1½ in. x 1½ in.). Draw and cut out a flame.

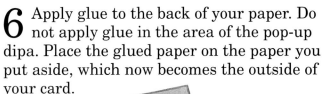

9 To make a wick, cut a piece of string 7.5 cm (3 in.) long. Glue one end of the string in the middle of the dipa. Put the other end of the string on the long edge of the dipa. Roll a small piece of tape so it is sticky on all sides. Place it on the end of the string. Press the flame shape on the end of the string so it is facing upward.

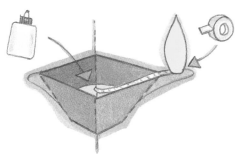

10 Write "Happy Diwali" inside the card, then decorate the inside and outside. If you wish, draw a string of small colored lights around the inside of the card. Colored lights are often used to decorate homes during Diwali.

More holidays

Hinamatsuri, the Dolls' Festival, is celebrated by Japanese girls on March 3. They dress in their best kimonos and display their collections of dolls to their friends.

1 To make a doll bookmark, cut the shape on the right out of bristol board and decorate it.

2 Turn to the Chanukah card on page 30 and follow steps 1 to 5. Tape the doll to one side of the pop-up strip. Follow step 11, but write "Happy Hinamatsuri" inside.

Glue patterned paper around the doll to make a kimono

Use a piece of ribbon to make a sash

Draw on hair and a face

Your heritage is an important part of you. Did you, your parents or grandparents come from another country to North America? If so, research the flags that go with your ancestry.

1 Turn to the Diwali card on page 24 and follow steps 1 to 4. Draw and color the appropriate flag on a piece of paper, 6 cm x 4.5 cm (2 ¼ in. x 1 ¾ in.). (If necessary, make two or more flags.) To make a flagpole, cut a strip of bristol board 3 cm x 7.5 cm (⅛ in. x 3 in.) and glue it on the left of the flag.

2 Glue the bottom of the flagpole inside the base from step 1. Follow steps 6 and 10 but write a message about your heritage.

Hi Grandad!

Let's Celebrate Our Heritage!

Part Three

Celebrate your faith

The many religions around the world have their own ways of celebrating special days. In this chapter you'll find out how to make pop-up cards for Buddhist, Christian, Greek Orthodox, Islamic and Jewish holidays, while discovering why these holidays are special.

There are many religious holidays that are important to other groups. For example, St. Nicholas Day on December 6 is celebrated by Dutch and German families. Julian Christmas on January 7 is an exciting occasion for people of the Ukrainian Orthodox faith and they celebrate with a holy supper. Other religious occasions are Samvatsari, the holiest day of the Jain year, and Jamshedi Navroz, which is a spring festival for Zoroastrian families. If your religion isn't represented here, adapt one of the cards in this chapter (or anywhere in the book) to celebrate your faith.

Celebrate Easter

The first Sunday following the first full moon after March 21 (the Spring Equinox). It's also the first Sunday after the Jewish Passover (a spring festival of freedom).

Easter is the most important holiday for Christians. They believe that on this day Jesus Christ, the Son of God, rose from his grave and came back to life. The cross on which Jesus was crucified and died is a symbol of Easter and so are hot cross buns, flowers, chickens — and of course eggs and bunnies. In many countries the Easter bunny brings kids Easter eggs and other treats.

1 Fold in half a piece of paper, 21.5 cm x 28 cm (8 ½ in. x 11 in.). Put it aside.

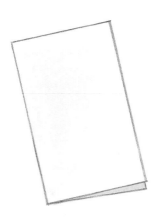

2 To make an egg for your Easter bunnies to hide behind, take a bright-colored piece of paper, 10 cm x 10 cm (4 in. x 4 in.). On this paper, draw a circle with a diameter of 6 to 8 cm (2 ¼ to 3 ⅛ in.). (Use a compass or trace around a can or lid.) Cut out the circle and decorate it.

3 Fold the circle in half. Fold it again so it is folded in quarters. Open the circle and mark where the folds cross with a dot. Starting at the outside edge of the circle, cut along one of the fold lines to the dot.

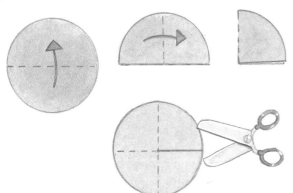

4 Place the circle so the cut line is at the bottom. Fold the top fold line into a mountain fold (see page 6). Fold the other two fold lines into mountain folds as shown. You now have two tabs at the bottom of the curved shape.

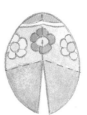

5 Open the paper you set aside in step 1. Apply glue to the bottom of the tabs of the curved shape, and place the shape near the top of the other paper. Be sure to match the middle fold line of the shape with the fold line of the paper. Press the shape in place. The tabs will overlap. If necessary, apply tape to the tabs to secure them.

6 To make the bunny and baby bunny, fold a white piece of paper, 21.5 cm x 28 cm (8 ½ in. x 11 in.), in half. Place it so the folded edge is on your left. Draw the following shapes along the folded edge. Cut them out. Add details such as eyes, a nose, whiskers and a mouth to the two bunnies.

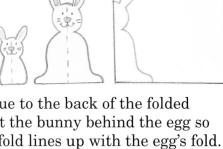

7 Fold the large bunny so the middle fold becomes a mountain fold. Fold the paws forward.

8 Apply glue to the back of the folded paws. Fit the bunny behind the egg so the bunny's fold lines up with the egg's fold. Press the bunny's paws to the front of the egg as shown.

9 Apply glue to the bottom half of the front of the baby bunny. Matching the fold lines, press the baby bunny against the back of the egg. Close the card and check to make sure nothing sticks out. If it does, reposition the bunnies.

10 Write an Easter greeting inside the card, then decorate the inside and outside.

HOPPY EASTER!

Celebrate Chanukah

Usually December (begins on the twenty-fifth day of the Hebrew month of Kislev)

Jews observe Chanukah, the Festival of Lights, to celebrate a miracle that took place in the Holy Land over 2100 years ago. A group of Jews had just defeated an invading army. To celebrate, they lit the lamp in the Temple. There was only enough oil for one day but it lasted for eight. During the eight days of Chanukah, families gather and each night use a *shammash* candle to light an additional candle in a candelabra called a *menorah*.

1 Take two pieces of paper, each 21.5 cm x 28 cm (8½ in. x 11 in.). Fold each paper in half. Put one aside.

2 In the middle of the folded edge of the other paper, mark two dots, 2 cm (¾ in.) apart.

3 Starting at the dots, draw 2 lines as shown. Each line should end about 2.5 cm (1 in.) from the folded edge of the page. The lines should be mirror images of each other. Cut the lines, starting from the folded edge.

4 Fold the cut section forward and then fold it back again.

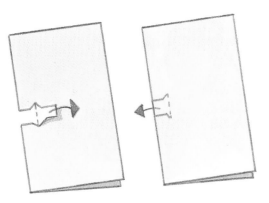

5 Open your card and hold it like a tent. Push the strip through to the other side of your card. Close the card and press firmly. Open it to see the pop-up strip.

6 Take a piece of paper, 5 cm x 10 cm (2 in. x 4 in.). Fold it in half. Place it so the folded edge is on your left.

7 Draw or trace the following menorah shape and cut it out.

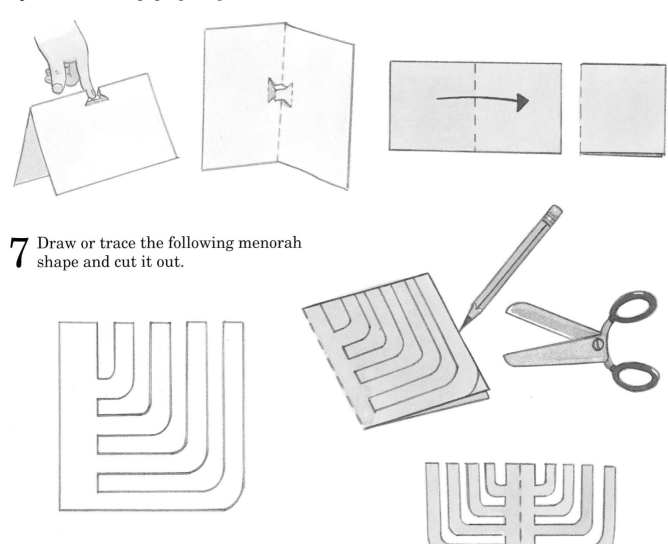

8 Draw nine candles with flames on a white piece of paper, 5 cm x 5 cm (2 in. x 2 in.). Color them and cut them out.

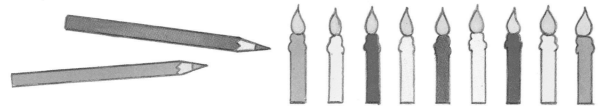

9 Apply glue on the top half of one side of the strip. Place the menorah shape on the glue as shown.

10 Apply glue to the candles and attach them to the menorah. The middle candle (the shammash) should be higher than the other candles. Shut your card and make sure no candles stick outside it. Reposition or trim your candles if necessary.

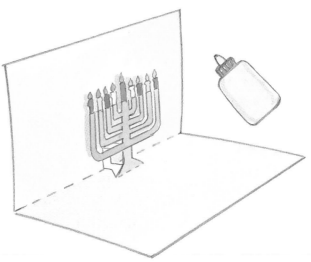

11 Apply glue to the back of your paper but not in the area of the pop-up. Place the glued paper on the paper you put aside, which now becomes the outside of your card. Write "Happy Chanukah" inside your card, then decorate the inside and outside.

Happy Chanukah

Celebrate Christmas

December 25

Christmas brings excitement each year for Christians everywhere. It celebrates the birth of Jesus Christ, the Son of God, almost 2000 years ago in a manger. In the story of Christ's birth, three kings, or Wise Men, brought him gold, frankincense (incense) and myrrh (perfume). Other symbols of Christmas are angels, holly, Santa Claus, reindeer and candy canes.

1 Fold in half a piece of paper, 35 cm x 30 cm (14 in. x 12 in.). Put it aside.

2 To make the Wise Man mask, take another piece of paper, 21.5 cm x 28 cm (8 ½ in. x 11 in.). Fold it in half and place it so the folded edge is on your left.

3 Mark a dot on the folded edge, 17 cm (7 in.) up from the bottom of the paper. Mark a second dot on the bottom of the paper, 12 cm (4 ¾ in.) from the fold.

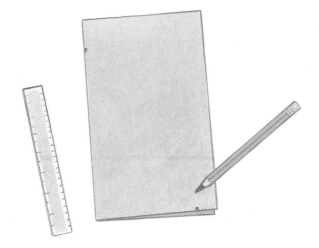

4 Between these dots, draw the following shape. Mark the dotted line as well. Cut out the shape. Save the remaining paper.

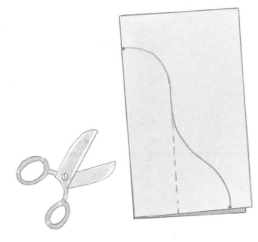

5 Fold the right edge toward the fold line along the dotted line.

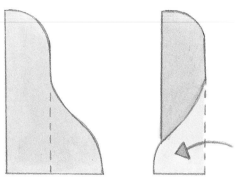

6 On the right folded edge of the shape, draw a line 2.5 cm (1 in.) long as shown. Cut along the line.

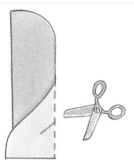

7 Fold the cut section down and press firmly. Fold the cut section back to its original position.

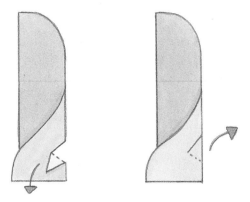

8 Open your large shape and turn it upside down. Bend the middle fold to create a mountain fold. Bend the side folds to create valley folds (see page 6). You now have two side flaps.

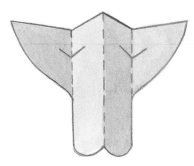

9 To make the small cut sections pop out, pull the shapes toward you and press along the fold lines. The shapes are the Wise Man's eyes. Fold the bottom half of the cut shapes upward as shown.

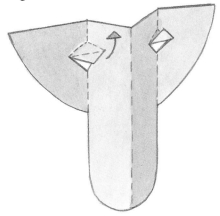

10 To make the nose, cut a piece of paper, 6 cm x 6 cm (2 ¼ in. x 2 ¼ in.), from the paper you saved in step 4. Fold it in half; then cut out the following shape. Fold back the top edges to create tabs. Apply glue to the tabs and place the nose on the middle fold of the mask as shown. Draw a mouth below the nose.

11 To make the crown, take a piece of yellow or gold-colored paper, 10 cm x 24 cm (4 in. x 9 ½ in.), and fold it in half. Draw the following shape along the fold and cut it out. Decorate the crown with stickers, glitter and sequins. Glue it onto the top of the Wise Man's head, matching the fold lines.

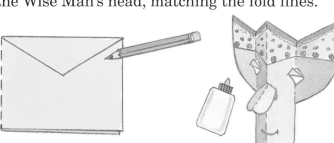

12 Make small holes on each side of the head, under the crown. Take two pieces of string, 30 cm (12 in.) long, and tie one through each hole.

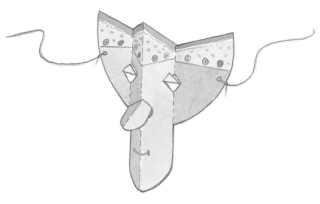

13 To attach your pop-up mask to the card, roll two pieces of tape so they are sticky on all sides. Place the tape on the back of the mask near the string holes. Open the piece of paper you put aside in step 1. Match the middle fold of the mask with the fold in the paper and press the mask down firmly. Write "Merry Christmas" inside your card, then decorate the inside and outside. When you want to use the mask, pull it off the card and remove the tape.

Other Ideas

To make a reindeer, use brown paper and follow steps 1 to 9. To make antlers, fold another piece of paper in half and draw the following shape and cut it out. Apply glue to the antlers and press them to the back of the head, near the top. Cut out a red nose and glue it to the snout. Punch small holes on each side of the head and attach pieces of string to make a mask. Follow step 13 to make a pop-up card.

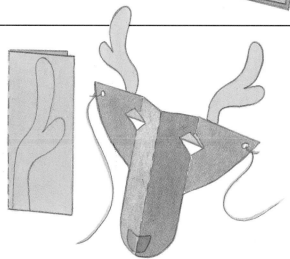

Celebrate Eid-ul-Fitre

Can occur any time of year according to a 36-year calendar cycle

Eid-ul-Fitre is a festival for Muslims, who follow Islam as their religion. It celebrates the end of Ramadan, the ninth month of the Islamic calendar, set aside for praying to Allah (God) and fasting. Eid-ul-Fitre is a time of giving presents, getting together with friends and family, and worshiping at the mosque. On the eve of Eid-ul-Fitre, Muslims look for the new moon to know when they can end their fast.

1 Take two pieces of paper, each 21.5 cm x 28 cm (8 ½ in. x 11 in.). Fold each paper in half. Put one aside.

2 Place the other paper so the folded edge is on your left. From the folded edge, draw two lines as shown. The lines should not reach farther than 6 cm (2 ¼ in.) from the folded edge. Cut the two lines, starting from the folded edge.

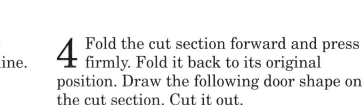

3 Fold the cut strip forward. Draw the following two solid lines and dotted line. Cut only the solid lines.

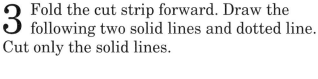

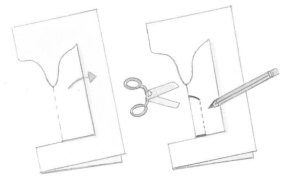

4 Fold the cut section forward and press firmly. Fold it back to its original position. Draw the following door shape on the cut section. Cut it out.

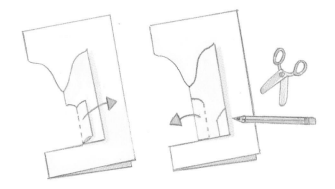

5 Open your paper. Bend the middle fold to create a mountain fold. Bend the folds beside the middle fold into valley folds. Bend the outside folds into mountain folds (see page 6).

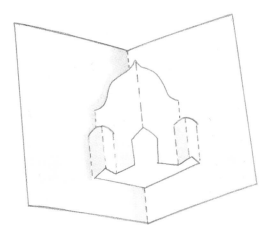

6 To make the minarets, or towers, take two pieces of paper, 5 cm x 10 cm (2 in. x 4 in.). Place one paper on top of the other paper and fold the papers in half as shown. Place the folded papers so the folded edges are on your left. Draw half of the minaret on the folded edge of the paper as shown. Cut out the shape.

7 Apply glue to the end of each shape. Place each minaret inside the outside structures as shown. Make sure the folds match.

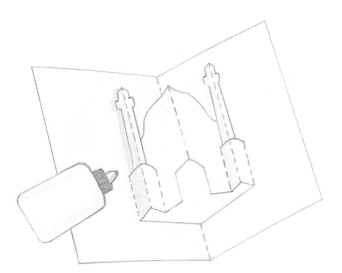

8 Apply glue to the back of your paper but not in the area of the cut shapes. Place the glued paper on the paper you put aside, which now becomes the outside of your card. Write "Eid Mubarak" or "Happy Eid Greeting" inside the card, then decorate the inside and outside.

Celebrate Wesak

Around the second Sunday in May. It is on the day of the fourth full moon after the lunar new year, or the Sunday closest to that day.

On Wesak, Buddhists around the world gather to celebrate the life of the prophet Buddha. During these celebrations people pray and meditate as well as feast, dance and sing. The baby Buddha in this card is in the position shown because when he was born he pointed to Heaven and Earth and said, "Above and below the Heavens, I am the World Honored One."

1 Fold in half a piece of paper, 21.5 cm x 28 cm (8 ½ in. x 11 in.). Put it aside.

2 To make the sacred lotus leaves that surround the baby Buddha, take a white piece of paper, 10 cm x 4 cm (4 in. x 1 ½ in.), and fold it in half. Place it so the folded edge is on your left.

3 Draw the following shape and cut it out. Fold the bottom edge up 1.2 cm (½ in.) Fold the bottom edge back to its original position.

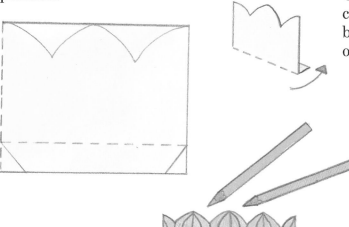

4 Open up the shape and draw the lines as shown. Color the bottom area of the leaves green and the top flower area pink. Create mountain folds (see page 6) along the center fold line and the fold line across the bottom. You now have two tabs at the bottom of your shape.

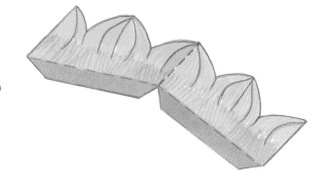

5 With your lotus folded in half, apply glue to the front of the left tab and then place the left side of the lotus face down on the base paper as shown. Press firmly.

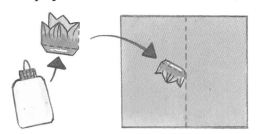

6 Apply glue to the front of the right tab and close your paper. Press the paper firmly.

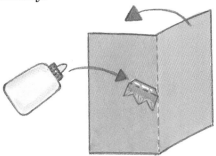

7 To make the baby Buddha, trace or photocopy the figure shown here. Color his robes yellow. (They are yellow because they are dyed with saffron, a valuable plant that gives a yellow color.) Cut out the figure and fold in half as shown.

8 Apply glue to the front bottom area of the baby Buddha's body. Match the fold lines of the baby Buddha to the fold lines of the lotus plant and press firmly.

9 To make cherry blossoms, take a pink piece of paper, 5 cm x 5 cm (2 in. x 2 in.), and fold it in half. Draw the four shapes shown along the folded edge. Cut them out. Glue these onto the base paper around the baby Buddha.

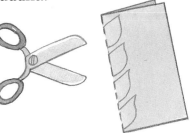

10 Write "Happy Wesak" inside your card, then decorate the inside and outside.

More holidays

La Navidad means "the nativity" and is the name for Christmas in Mexico. Each year between December 16 and December 24 people set up *nacimientos,* which are scenes showing Christ's birth, or nativity.

1 Turn to the Valentine's Day card on page 8 and follow steps 1 to 7 to make pop-up strips.

2 Draw and color the figures shown and glue each on the front of a strip. Follow step 12 to put a front and back on your card. Write "Feliz Navidad y Prospero Año Nuevo," which means "Merry Christmas and Happy New Year," inside your card, then decorate the inside and outside.

Orthodox Easter is a time for Orthodox Christians to rejoice that Christ has risen from the dead (see page 28 for more on Easter and when it occurs). Christians believe that Christ brings light and love to all. In the Greek Orthodox Church, during a midnight service on the day before Easter, the priest lights a candle and the light is passed to everyone there.

1 Turn to the Rosh Hashanah card on page 42 and follow steps 1 to 4. Draw and color a child around the pop-up face and hands. Draw, color and cut out a small candle in a paper cup. Glue the cup to the child's hands. Draw and color a priest and other worshipers with the child.

2 Follow step 10 but write "Christ is Risen!" inside the card.

Part Four

Celebrate the new year

Many cultures have a different day for celebrating the New Year. The timing varies because people throughout the world follow different calendars. Calendars that have January 1 as New Year's Day are called Gregorian calendars. They are 365 days long and are named after the man who created them. Other calendars follow the phases of the moon (lunar calendars) and some follow the sun (solar calendars). For instance, the Chinese calendar is lunar. The Jewish calendar is both solar and lunar. Other people who follow a lunar and solar calendar include Tibetans and Vietnamese. The Bahá'í calendar begins on March 21 and is a solar calendar. Native celebrations mark seasonal changes rather than calendar dates.

In all cultures, the new year begins with hope for a new start and a better year ahead. Have fun making different New Year's cards!

Celebrate Rosh Hashanah (Jewish New Year)

Usually September (the beginning of the Hebrew month of Tishri)

Rosh Hashanah is the Jewish New Year and marks the beginning of a ten-day celebration filled with prayer and worship. During religious services, the ram's horn, or *shofar,* is blown. The shofar has been used since biblical times and is blown only on historical and important occasions.

1 Take two pieces of paper, each 21.5 cm x 28 cm (8 ½ in. x 11 in.). Fold each paper in half. Put one aside.

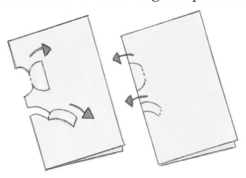

2 Place the other paper so the folded edge is on your left. From the folded edge draw two curved lines. This will become the shofar player's head. From the folded edge, draw two more curved lines as shown. These lines will be the arms. Make sure no lines reach more than 7 cm (2 ¾ in.) from the folded edge.

3 Cut all the lines, starting at the folded edge. Fold the cut sections forward, then fold them back to their original positions.

4 Open your paper and hold it like a tent. Push the cut sections through to the other side of your paper. Close the paper and press firmly. Open it to see the pop-up head and arms.

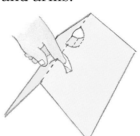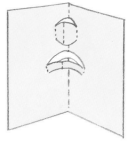

5 Draw and color the player's face and body. Cut along the fold line in the middle of the arms.

6 Draw or trace the following hand shape onto a folded piece of paper. Cut it out to make two hands and color them.

7 Apply glue behind the end of each arm as shown. Place a hand on each glued area. Secure the hands with tape.

8 Draw or trace the following shofar shape and cut it out. Color it on both sides.

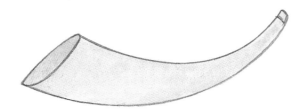

9 Apply glue to the palms of the hands. Place the shofar between the hands and press together. When you open and close the card, the shofar goes up and down. Adjust the position of the shofar if it is not moving properly.

10 Apply glue to the back of your paper but not in the area of the pop-up strips. Place the glued paper on the paper you put aside, which now becomes the outside of your card. Write "Rosh Hashanah Greetings" or "Shana Tova," which means "Good Year," inside your card, then decorate the inside and outside.

Celebrate New Year's Eve

December 31

This is one of the oldest and most widely celebrated festivals in the world. Some families go to church on New Year's Eve and pray for a peaceful and happy New Year. Other people go to parties and wait with excitement for midnight. When the clock strikes 12:00, they shout "Happy New Year!" and make lots of noise with horns and noisemakers.

1 Fold in half a piece of paper, 21.5 cm x 28 cm (8½ in. x 11 in.). Put it aside.

2 To make the bird for the cuckoo clock, take a piece of paper, 14 cm x 2.5 cm (5½ in. x 1 in.). Fold it in half crosswise and then fold it in half crosswise again so it is folded in quarters as shown.

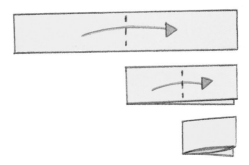

3 Fold the strip so the middle fold is a mountain fold and the side folds are valley folds (see page 6). Apply glue to the bottom of each side section.

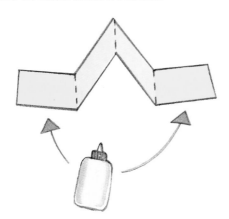

4 Take the paper you put aside. Hold the folded strip over the middle of the paper so the fold lines match. Press the glued sections down evenly on either side of the fold as shown. Close your paper and press firmly. When you open it you will have pop-up legs.

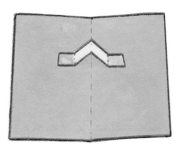

5 To make the wings, take a strip of paper, 23 cm x 4 cm (9 in. x 1½ in.). Fold it into quarters. Cut a scalloped edge as shown. Open your strip and fold it so the middle fold is a mountain fold and the side folds are valley folds.

6 Apply glue to both sides of the top of the pop-up legs. Place the scalloped strip onto the glued areas as shown. The end sections of the scalloped strip are the bird's wings.

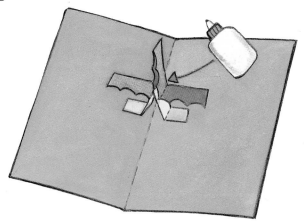

7 Cut out two strips of paper, each 7.5 cm x 2.5 cm (3 in. x 1 in.). Fold one strip into thirds so each section is 2.5 cm (1 in.) long. Repeat with the other strip.

8 Hold one folded strip so the ends are on the right. Apply glue to both ends as shown. Place it under the left wing near the middle fold of the paper.

9 Hold the other folded strip so the ends are on the left. Apply glue to both ends as shown. Place it under the right wing near the middle fold of the paper.

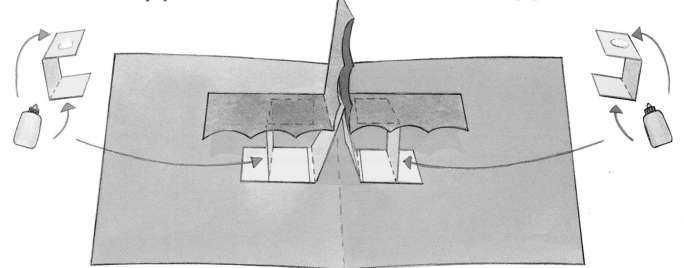

10 To make the beak of the bird, take a piece of paper, 14 cm x 10 cm (5½ in. x 4 in.), and fold it in half. Place it so the folded edge is on your left. Draw the following beak shapes along the folded edge. Cut out the beaks.

11 Apply glue to one end section of a beak. Place it in the top area of the bird's head and press them together firmly. Apply glue to the end section of the other beak. Place it below the first beak inside the paper strip so the beak is wide open. Press it firmly in place.

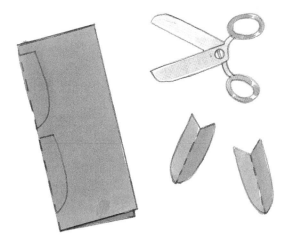

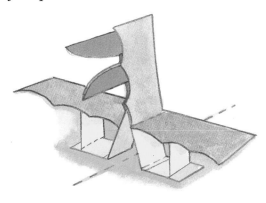

12 To make eyes, draw dots or use stickers on each side of the head. Add further decorations such as real or paper tail feathers. You can make a small horn by rolling a cone of paper. Or make a miniature noisemaker by rolling a small cylinder of paper and then curving the end of it. Glue one or both on the ends of the bird's wings.

13 Around the bird, draw a cuckoo clock for the bird to "pop" out of. Decorate the outside of the card and write a New Year greeting on the inside.

Celebrate Sun Nin (Chinese New Year)

Between January 21 and February 20, starting on the first day of the second new moon after the winter solstice; lasts for more than a week

Chinese New Year is a time for friends and family to visit each other. Red is considered a very lucky color. The New Year's Eve feast is served on a table covered with a red cloth and lit with red candles. Children receive small red envelopes containing money. There are also parades, often led by long, brightly decorated dragons.

1 To make the dragon's head, take two different colored pieces of paper, each 21.5 cm x 28 cm (8½ in. x 11 in.). Fold each paper in half. Put one aside.

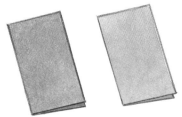

2 Place the other paper so the folded edge is on your left. Mark a dot 8 cm (3⅛ in.) from the bottom of the paper.

3 From this dot, draw a curved line as shown. The final point of the curved line should be 6 cm (2¼ in.) from the folded edge. Cut the line.

4 From the end of the curved line, draw a diagonal dotted line toward the folded edge of the paper.

5 Fold the cut piece up along the dotted line. Press the fold firmly. Fold the cut piece down to its original position again.

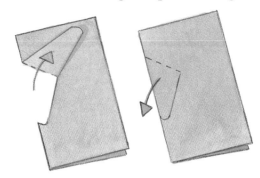

6 Open your paper and hold it like a tent. Push the cut piece down in the opposite direction of the fold so it is pushed through to the other side of the paper. Close the paper and press firmly. When you open your paper, a dragon's snout will pop out.

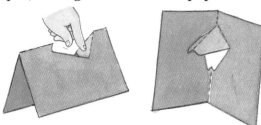

47

7 To make the pop-out eyes, close the paper. On the upper folded edge of the pop-up snout, mark two dots, 1.2 cm (½ in.) apart. Starting at the dots, draw two parallel lines, 1 cm (⅜ in.) long. Cut the two lines, cutting through both folded edges of the pop-up snout.

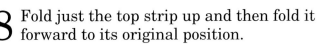
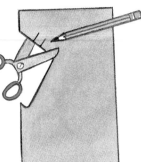

8 Fold just the top strip up and then fold it forward to its original position.

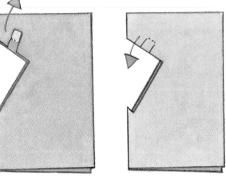

9 Open your paper and push the strip down and through to the other side. Close your paper and press firmly.

10 Place your paper so the fold line is on the right. Fold the cut strip, then fold it down to its original position.

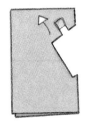
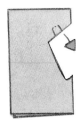

11 Open your paper and push the strip down and through to the other side. You will now have a pair of eyes.

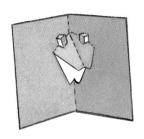

12 Close your paper slightly, then reach inside it and fold the tip of the snout to one side as shown. Fold the tip back to its original position, then push down on it to create extra folds on the snout. The folds make the snout point down.

13 Apply glue to the back of your paper but not in the area of the eyes or snout. Place the glued paper on the paper you put aside, which now becomes the outside of your card.

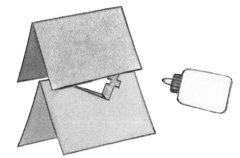

48

14 Carefully cut around the dragon's head as shown, cutting through the two layers of paper. Apply extra glue between the layers of paper if needed. Do not apply glue in the pop-up areas.

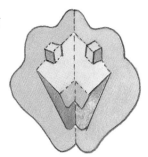

15 Add details by drawing on nostrils and scales. To make teeth, glue small triangles of paper along the inside edge of the snout. To decorate the head, attach strips of colored paper.

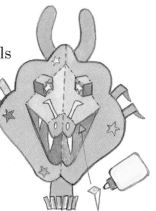

16 To make the body of the dragon, take a colored piece of paper, 21.5 cm x 28 cm (8½ in. x 11 in.), and fold it in half lengthwise. Open it and cut it along the fold line.

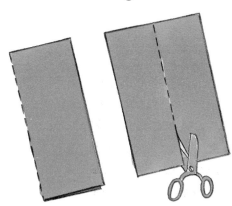

17 Overlap the two pieces slightly and glue them together. Draw a line as shown and cut the line. Print on the paper "Sun Nin Chun Po," which means "Progressive New Year." Decorate the body. If you like, add stickers or a fringe of paper along the bottom edge.

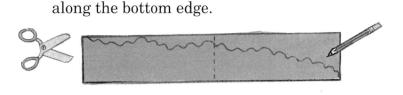

Sun Nin Chun Po

18 Accordion fold (see page 6) the body as shown. Apply glue to the front of the first fold of the body section. Glue it to the back of the dragon's head as shown.

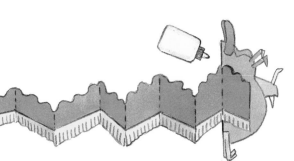

19 Fold up the dragon and send it as a card. You can also add strings to the top of the dragon and hang it from the ceiling or the top of a window.

Sun Nin Chun Po

Celebrate Noruz

From March 21 to April 2

Noruz means "New Day" and is a very old spring festival. It is the national holiday of Iran and is also celebrated in other areas in the Middle East once known as Persia, such as Afghanistan and Iraq. Preparations for Noruz include housecleaning, growing *sabzeh* (wheat or lentil sprouts) and setting a special New Year's table.

1 Take one piece of paper, 21.5 cm x 28 cm (8 ½ in. x 11 in.). Fold it in half.

2 Take another piece of paper, 15 cm x 15 cm (6 in. x 6 in.). Fold it in half top to bottom. Fold it again so it is folded in quarters.

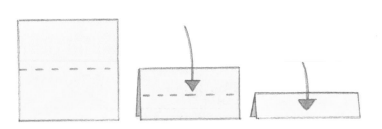

3 Fold your piece of paper as shown so each fold is a mountain fold (see page 6).

4 Apply glue to the back of the top section. Place this glued section in the middle of the bottom half of your paper as shown. The top edge of this glued piece should be 5 cm (2 in.) from the middle fold line.

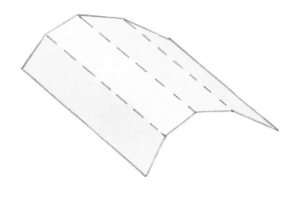

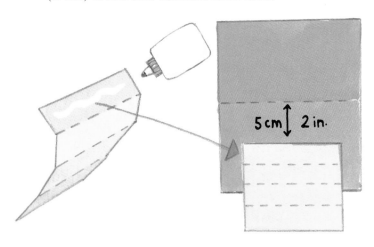

5 Fold the section in half as shown. Place a clear piece of tape along the top edge.

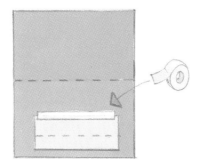

6 Draw and color a row of brown seeds along the bottom edge of the folded section.

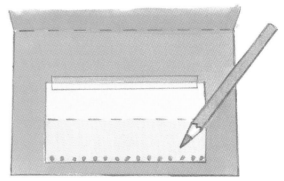

7 To create a tab, take a piece of paper, 1.2 cm x 5 cm (½ in. x 2 in.). Print "Pull" at the top. Apply glue to the back of the tab, at the bottom, and place it on the folded section, under the middle fold.

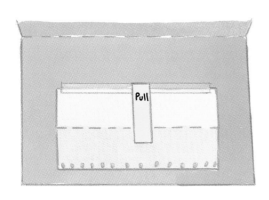

8 Pull the tab so the section moves upward. Draw green sprouts (the sabzeh) beneath the seeds. Draw and color a plate under the sprouts and a red ribbon around the middle of the sprouts.

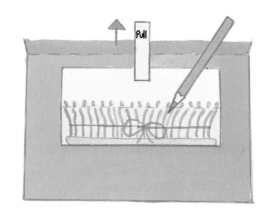

9 Push the tab down so the section is folded in half as shown. Write "Happy Noruz" at the top of your card, then decorate the inside and outside. If you like, include a little bag of lentils or wheat seeds in your card. If the lentils are placed in a dish and kept moist, they will sprout.

More holidays

Hogmanay is what Scottish people call January 1. The name means "New Year with Mistletoe." One Hogmanay custom is to watch for the "first foot," the first person to enter the home on New Year's Day. It is good luck for your first foot to be a dark-haired man and bad luck if he is red-haired.

1 Follow steps 1 to 4 of the Groundhog Day card on page 58 but don't glue a piece of paper to the strip.

2 Draw, color and cut out a small man and attach him to the end of the strip. Draw the scene as shown so the man walks in the door.

3 Follow step 9, but write "Happy Hogmanay" inside.

Baisakhi is celebrated by Sikhs, Buddhists, Jains and Hindus. It occurs on April 13 (or April 14 once every 36 years). For Sikhs, Baisakhi is a harvest festival and also marks the birth of the Sikh nation in 1699. At that time five Sikhs were baptized into the religion and became *khalsa* or "perfect men." Orange and white are the colors of the Sikh flag.

1 Turn to the Chanukah card on page 30 and follow steps 1 to 5 using orange paper.

2 Trace or photocopy the symbol of the Sikh faith shown here onto white paper and cut it out. Glue the symbol to the front of the strip. Follow step 11 but write "Happy Baisakhi" inside the card and decorate the inside and outside.

Part Five

Celebrate people and events

If you want to find out about some interesting people and special occasions, then this is the chapter for you. For instance, you'll find pop-up card ideas for Martin Luther King Day and St. Patrick's Day. Those are just two of the people who are celebrated around the world with their own special day. Christopher Columbus is remembered on the second Monday in October and Scottish people celebrate the poet Robbie Burns on January 25. There are also lots of saints' days, including St. Thomas Day, St. Ann's Day and St. Basil's Day.

Some special occasions have been celebrated for a very long time, such as Halloween and Groundhog Day. Others have been around for a much shorter time, such as Veterans' Day and Earth Day. You can celebrate any of these occasions by sending a pop-up card to someone special.

Celebrate St. Patrick's Day

March 17

St. Patrick's Day is the anniversary of the death of the Irish saint St. Patrick. On this day it is a custom to wear green whether you are Irish or not. Some of the symbols for St. Patrick's Day are shamrocks, harps, pipes, leprechauns and pots of gold.

1 Take two pieces of paper, each 21.5 cm x 28 cm (8½ in. x 11 in.). One paper should be white and the other green. Fold each paper in half. Put the green one aside.

2 Place the white paper so that the folded edge is on your left. Fold it again so it is folded in quarters. Open the paper so it is folded in half. Take the top left corner and fold it down to the center line.

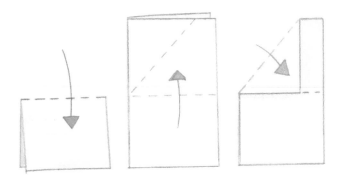

3 Open the paper, so it is folded in half again. Take the top left corner and fold forward to the diagonal fold line. Press the folds firmly.

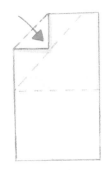

4 Open your paper. Draw and color a rainbow as shown.

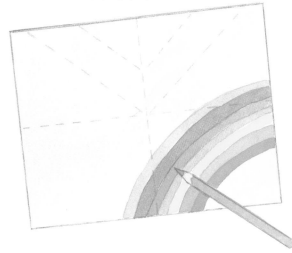

5 You will see two upside-down triangles at the top of your page. Pull the large triangle toward you. Press the fold lines so the triangle points forward.

6 Take the top small triangle and press the folds so it is pushed away from you as shown.

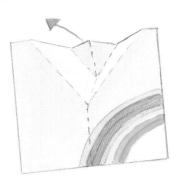

7 To make a leprechaun, take a piece of paper, 10 cm x 10 cm (4 in. x 4 in.), and fold it in half. Draw the leprechaun figure shown along the folded edge and cut it out. Open the figure, color it and add details. Apply glue to the middle of the back of the leprechaun. Press it onto the top small triangle, matching the fold lines.

8 To make a pot of gold, take a piece of paper, 4 cm x 4 cm (1½ in. x 1½ in.), and fold it in half. Draw the following shape along the folded edge. Cut it out and open it up. Color it and add details. Apply glue to the back of the pot. Glue it onto the bottom of your paper, matching the fold lines.

9 Apply glue to the back of your paper as shown but not in the area of the pop-up triangles. Place the glued paper on the paper you put aside, which now becomes the outside of your card. Write a St. Patrick's Day message inside the card, then decorate the inside and outside.

Celebrate Halloween

October 31

Halloween is a time for dressing up in costumes, going trick-or-treating and telling spooky stories. For hundreds of years, people believed Halloween was a night when witches and ghosts really walked the earth. The name Halloween comes from the name All Hallows' Eve. Hallows is an old word that means "saints," and November 1 is All Hallows' Day or All Saints' Day.

1 Take one black and one white piece of paper, each 21.5 cm x 28 cm (8½ in. x 11 in.). Fold each paper in half. Put the black paper aside.

2 Place the white piece of paper so the folded edge is on your left. Mark a dot 7 cm (2¾ in.) from the bottom of the paper.

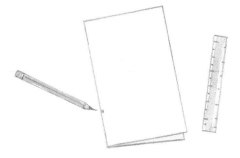

3 From this dot, draw a diagonal line, 7.5 cm (3 in.) long, as shown. Cut the line. From the end of the line, draw a diagonal dotted line toward the folded edge of the paper as shown. The dotted line should end 5 cm (2 in.) from the top of the paper.

4 Fold the cut piece up along the dotted line. Press the fold firmly. Fold the cut piece down to its original position again.

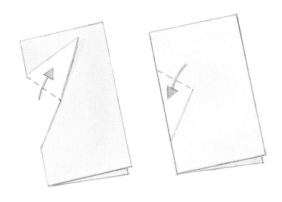

5 Open your paper and hold it like a tent. Push the cut piece down in the opposite direction of the fold so it is pushed through to the other side of the paper. Close the paper and press firmly. When you open your paper, you will see a pop-up shape. This is the bat's head.

6 To make bat ears, take a piece of white paper. Draw a circle with a diameter of 9 cm (3½ in.). (Use a compass or trace around a can or lid.) Cut out the circle.

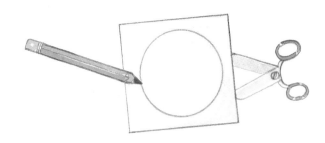

7 Fold the circle in half, then in quarters and finally into eighths. Open up the circle. Cut out one-quarter of the circle, cutting along the fold lines. Cut the remaining part of the circle in half, cutting along a fold line.

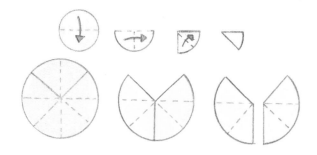

8 Apply glue to the bottom section of each piece. Press the pieces firmly on either side of the bat's head. Draw eyes on the sections at the top of the head and a nose at the bottom of the head. Cut out triangular teeth from white paper, fold them as shown and draw blood on their tips. Glue them inside the bat's mouth. Draw the bat's body as shown. Color your bat.

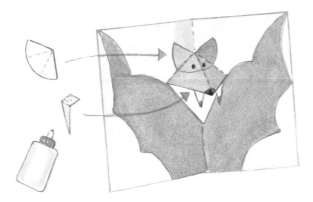

9 Apply glue to the back of your paper but not in the area of the bat's head. Place the glued paper on the paper you put aside, which now becomes the outside of your card. Write a Halloween message inside your card, then decorate the inside and outside.

Celebrate Groundhog Day

February 2

On Groundhog Day, the groundhog pops its head out of its hole. If the sun is shining, the groundhog sees its shadow. That scares it into its hole and six more weeks of winter are supposed to follow. If the groundhog doesn't see its shadow, spring comes soon. Two famous North American groundhogs are Wiarton Willie of Wiarton, Ontario, in Canada and Punxsutawney Phil of Punxsutawney, Pennsylvania, in the United States.

1 Take two pieces of paper, each 21.5 cm x 28 cm (8 ½ in. x 11 in.). One piece of paper should be white and the other one colored. Fold each paper in half. Put the colored one aside.

2 Take the white piece of paper and open it up. In the center of the right side of the paper, mark a dot 8 cm (3 ⅛ in.) from the top of the page as shown. From this dot, draw a horizontal line 4 cm (1 ½ in.) long. Cut the line with a cutting blade or a pair of pointed scissors.

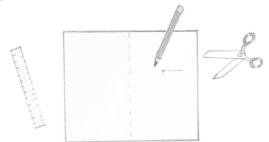

3 Measure 7.5 cm (3 in.) down from the cut line. Draw and cut another line, 4 cm (1 ½ in.) long, directly below the other line as shown.

4 Cut a strip of white bristol board, 14 cm x 2 cm (5 ½ in. x ¾ in.). Take a piece of paper, 2.5 cm x 2.5 cm (1 in. x 1 in.). Draw, color and cut out a small rock. Glue only the top part of the rock to the end of the strip. The rock should completely cover the end of the strip.

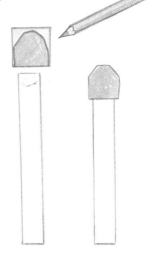

5 Draw and color the top half of a groundhog below the rock on the bristol board as shown.

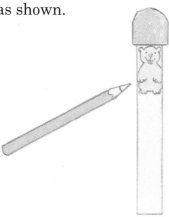

6 Slide the blank end of the strip into the top slot, then down and back out the bottom slot.

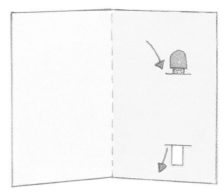

7 Cut out a thin rectangle of bristol board, 5 cm x .6 cm (2 in. x ¼ in.). Push the bottom of the strip up so the groundhog is showing above the slot. Turn the paper over. Draw a line at the top of the strip.

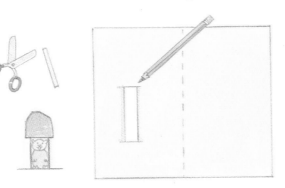

8 Pull the strip down farther. Place the rectangle of bristol board so the long edge lies along the line and tape it in place. Turn the paper over. When you push the strip up, the groundhog should appear. When you pull it down, you see only a rock.

9 Apply glue to the back of your paper but not in the area of the sliding strip. Place the glued paper on the paper you put aside, which now becomes the outside of your card. On the inside of the card draw a snow scene and write "Happy Groundhog Day." Decorate the outside of the card.

Celebrate Earth Day

April 22

The first Earth Day took place in 1970 in the United States. Today it is a global event with over 90 countries involved. Earth Day events have made people more aware of the fragile environment. Activities include cleanup and recycling projects, concerts related to the environment, composting and outdoor walks.

1 Take two pieces of paper, each 21.5 cm x 28 cm (8½ in. x 11 in.). One paper should be white and the other green. Fold each paper in half. Put the green paper aside.

2 Place the white paper so the folded edge is on your left. Mark a dot 5 cm (2 in.) from the top of the paper. Mark a dot 5 cm (2 in.) from the bottom of the paper. From these dots draw curved lines as shown. The lines should not reach farther than 6 cm (2¼ in.) from the folded edge.

3 Under the top curved line, draw the following two curved lines, each about 1 cm (⅜ in.) apart. The two top lines should meet as shown.

4 Starting above the bottom curved line, draw the following curved lines, each about 1 cm (⅜ in.) apart. The two bottom lines should meet as shown.

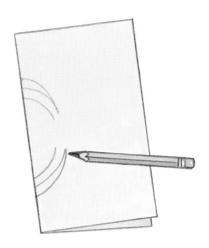

5 Cut all of the lines, starting from the folded edge. Remove the two cut pieces.

6 Fold the entire middle section to the right. Fold the smaller inner section to the left.

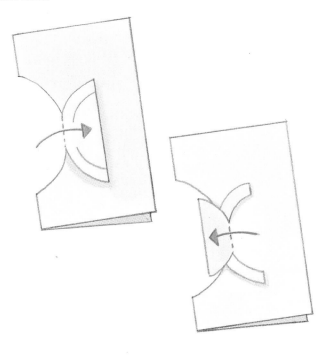

7 Fold the sections back to their original positions. Open your paper and hold it like a tent. Push only the middle section down, in the opposite direction of the fold so it is pushed through to the other side of your paper. Close your paper, with the cut section inside, and press firmly. Open your paper. The round middle section will stand out. This section represents the Earth.

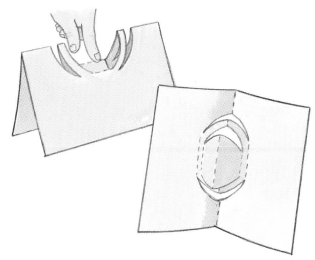

8 Draw and color the Earth as shown. It is easier to color the Earth if you put a piece of paper under the cut sections.

9 Draw and color the two children as shown with their hands meeting in the middle.

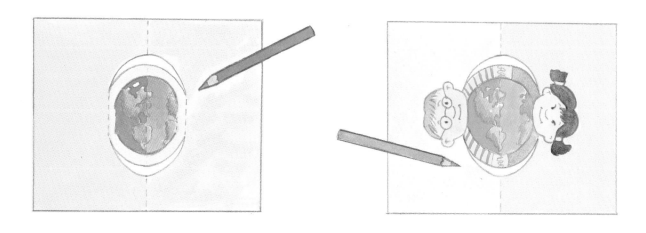

10 Apply glue to the back of your paper. Glue it to the green paper, which now becomes the outside of your card. Do not apply glue in the area of the Earth. You can apply a small amount of glue under the hands. Write an Earth Day message inside the card, then decorate the inside and outside.

Together We Can Help The Environment

HAPPY EARTH DAY!

More holidays

Martin Luther King Day is celebrated on January 15, the day this great man was born, or the Monday closest to it. He was an African American and his hope was that one day people would treat each other equally, no matter what their color. In 1964 Dr. King won the Nobel Peace Prize but in 1968 he was assassinated.

1 Follow steps 1 to 7 of the Valentine's Day card on page 8 but make only three strips as shown. On two small pieces of paper draw doves with olive branches as symbols of peace. Color and cut them out. On another piece of paper, write the word "PEACE." Glue the pieces of paper to the pop-up strips as shown.

2 Follow step 12 but write "Peace on Martin Luther King Day" inside the card, then decorate the inside and outside.

Veterans' Day takes place on November 11. At the eleventh hour of the eleventh day of the eleventh month of each year, people remember Americans who died in war or on peacekeeping missions.

1 Follow steps 1 to 6 of the Mother's Day card on page 10. To make poppies, take three squares of white paper, 6 cm x 6 cm (2¼ in. x 2¼ in.). Draw, color and cut out three poppies and glue one to the front of each pop-up section.

2 Follow step 8 but write a Veterans' Day message inside the card, then decorate the inside and outside.

63

Celebrate with pop-up cards all year long

Here are all the holidays in this book, listed in the order they occur during the year.